MOMENTS OF TRUTH

The challenge of coming face to face with life

Time, slipping through your fingers like grains of sand. At first there seems so much time, doesn't there? Time enough to squander even. As the years pass there seems to have been so very little time really. There are so very few days in our life and each moment gets more and more precious. Treasure each second.

Ray Moore

D o you sometimes have the experience of being so filled with energy that you feel you could achieve anything you put your mind to – and sometimes of its opposite, when it seems as if the current has been switched off and nothing appears to be worthwhile? In this book, people describe experiences which have these characteristics. The writers were asked if they would be willing to tell others of times when some event stopped them in their tracks and challenged them to think about what was *really* of worth to them, and why that was so.

Often we go through experiences by ourselves. It seems difficult to talk about them. Maybe sometime later it comes as a relief to discover that others have had similar experiences. We need not have had that sense of isolation. In a recent discussion, a group of sixteen-year-olds talked about this. Suzanne said: "People need to think more about serious things – like death, dying, how things change – then they might feel more relaxed about them." By publishing this book, Ely Cathedral Publications Group is inviting the discussion to continue. Life brings human beings face to face with many different challenges. How do people respond to them and what do they discover by coping with them?

A cathedral is a place of worship. Why should it be concerned with these matters of everyday life? "I don't see the link," said Francesca, who was in Suzanne's discussion group. Well, what *is* worship? Have you noticed that people find different ways of expressing themselves when they feel strongly, even passionately, about something? These strong feelings may influence their work or their creation of a home and family; they may be expressed through personal skills, perhaps in sport, through playing an instrument or in being able to communicate well with others. It seems that each of us is capable of enormous energy when we feel that something is worth doing and that, perhaps, *we* can do it. This output of energy is the human recognition of worth and our response to it, or our *worship*. The words come from the Old English weorth (worth) and weorthscipe (worship). Do you think this explains the link between worship and everyday life that Francesca couldn't see?

For some people certain experiences, which are powerful and deeply felt, seem to point beyond the present moment to some hidden truth, a truth they cannot fully grasp. This they may wish to acknowledge in a *place* of worship – think of the energy that went into the building of Ely Cathedral. Although others may not be led to respond in this way, all of us who experience this sense of worth, and sometimes its loss, find it affects our understanding of life and time, and we wonder about its meaning:

> When, as a child, I laughed and wept, time crept.
> When as a youth, I dreamed and talked, time walked.
> When I became a full-grown man, time ran.
> And later, as I older grew, time flew.
> Soon shall I find, while travelling on, time gone.

The Cathedral plans to publish a short series of books on worship. This, the first in the series, explores the question, What *is* worship? through the writings of people between the ages of ten and seventy-eight years. The five lines of the verse about time correspond to the five sections of the book and guide the reader through the experiences described. The thread of time links the experiences and shows how they change. What has each writer discovered to be of worth, to be *true*, as a result of coming face to face with life's experiences? Can *you* recall times when moments of truth have come to you?

CONTENTS

When, as a child,
I laughed
and wept,
time crept.

At the age of ten there seemed to be so much time. If you were waiting for something you badly wanted to happen, time could seem endless. Happenings could be great fun, magically happy or unbearably painful. People sometimes tell you things won't hurt so much when you are older. Certainly, as a child, one may not have many resources to draw on when things are hard, as some of the writings which follow make clear. What are some of the causes of joy and sorrow for the children writing in this section? What are the things that matter most to them?

. . . as a child . . .

Growing old

It all started long ago. We had a dog but it got run over so we got a puppy. We called it Trudy. I used to put my cars in a row and she would get a car, carry it away and put it down again somewhere else. She chased cats out of the garden and protected me. If someone was beating me up she would bark at them. Now she is getting old, and her back legs are going.

. . . as a child . . .

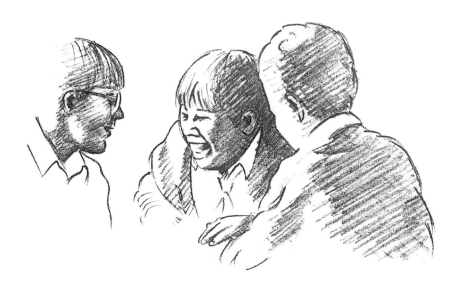

Being different

When I was eight I moved from Scotland to England. Three weeks after I moved my friends sent me letters to tell me what was happening in Scotland. I missed all my friends. When I got to England, everyone made fun of me because I had an accent. I'll never forget what it was like. It took me a year to adapt to my new surroundings. After that I said I'd never make fun of someone because of their accent or because they're different.

Family holiday

It was great when we went to Center Parcs with my sisters' families – Jo's, Sharon's and Lucinda's. The swimming pool was very big and there were lots of water slides. My favourite part of the swimming pool was the wild rapids. Our bungalow had three bedrooms, one shower and a spa bath. There were lots of shops and a big pond with ducks, fish and terrapins in it, and that was all under the dome. We went Ten-Pin Bowling and that was really good because I beat my "brain-box" sister, and I beat her at Table-Tennis and at Crazy Golf. On our last day we had a ride on the Peddlows. After that we went for a bike-ride. Mum spotted a nest of baby Adders. Then they slithered away under a low hanging bough of a tree.

The road accident

My friend went home on the bus and that day I was going with her. The journey was fine until we came to a corner. All the other children knew something was happening in front. I saw two cars, one in the ditch, the other the wrong way round on the road.

The police, ambulance and firemen were there. All the thirty odd children on the bus knew what had happened. One of the other girls noticed that one of the cars belonged to another girl's father. When the girl knew this she burst into tears and started calling for her dad.

One of the older girls tried to comfort her but it did not work. My friend and I could not stop talking about it when I was around her house.

I felt so sorry for her. I did not know what to think or feel. I was so glad that it was not my dad that was in the accident.

A memory

A memory which has stayed with me for a year and two months. My mum called the whole family to sit in the living-room. I was mucking around and said "Bad news or good?"

Mum said "Bad."
So I said "What is it?"

She paused then said that she was getting a divorce and dad was leaving in half an hour. I felt suddenly weird all over and screamed out "No!" I started crying. I was very hurt. I just couldn't cope. I felt like dying. I said stupid things out of anger because they'd promised never to split up. I was still crying when dad had to leave. I said "Goodbye", and he left. I was crying for three hours. I didn't sleep for two nights. Then dad had an affair with a lady he was staying with. After a few months he went off with an American lady.

I changed. It made me say things and get beaten up and I got very hurt by people teasing. I remember everything.

. . . as a child . . .

I am very lucky

The best day of my life was the day I was born, 30th November 1979. Although I cannot remember this day it must have been a joyful one celebrating my birth.

I have had many happy times since my first birthday; for example spending time with family and pets, going on holiday and even going to school.

I think I am very lucky because I have a lovely home, three sisters and a stupid brother. I also have brilliant parents, which most people do not have. I am happy that I am alive today.

When, as a youth,
I dreamed
and talked,
time walked.

'As a youngster, I had all sorts of plans and ambitions about what I was going to do and become', recalls a writer in the **Travelling On** section. There is pleasure in dreaming, in achieving – "when you've done something and you know you've done it well", as a 15-year-old boy said, and in talking with friends – 'We're all very close and discuss everything', says a writer in this section. Others thought maturing and independence brought problems – 'the responsibilities and worries of becoming a fully instated member of the working community', and the fact that 'if you are a "different kind of person" you can be rejected and isolated from people you want to get on with'. How do experiences change at this stage? What do they do to us? Do we know *now* what is most important to us?

. . . as a youth . . .

Home

I get aggressive at home. I hit doors and don't feel welcome there.

If my mother is there and it possesses love I know it's home.

School

I enjoy school and like the safety of it and the challenges and the friends I have made.

I think the worst part of being at school is when you are on your own.

Myself

I enjoy to listen to loud music. It relaxes me and takes out the tension within me. Lying on my bed gives me a bigger chance to think things through and take a look at myself, other people, other things.

I enjoy the quietness of being on my own – no one to speak to – not having to make the effort to speak.

Friends

I love the company of my friends and now we are all very close and discuss everything. I also feel that your friends make you feel good about yourself – I don't know how though!

With friends you feel needed because they ask you how you feel and are interested in what you think.

What kind of person am I?

As my life progresses I find myself learning from the many new experiences I come across nearly every day. Not every experience is unusual, memorable or even particularly interesting, yet each one helps to build up my life. Every time I encounter something unfamiliar I have to deal with it in my own way, thus increasing my scope of knowledge and understanding.

I believe that as the days pass I am discovering and uncovering more and more about myself, breaking down barriers and continuously setting myself new goals to achieve. Challenges and demanding tasks are vital in my life because I like to constantly test myself to find out where my limits are and what kind of person I am.

There are rare occasions in some people's lives when they experience thoughts and feelings which they've never even contemplated before the unique moment occurs. A certain spontaneous, or, perhaps, premeditated event can create uncontrollable emotions that can't be kept back or held in. These moments are very special yet unfortunately infrequent. This is possibly why they have such a striking effect.

I had one such moving experience three years ago. At that time I participated a great deal in Judo competitions and general training. This particular incident happened at a grading where I was supposed to be changing from my junior brown belt to a senior brown belt. I won all my fights to gain my brown belt and was then told I was to have a line-up of three women whom I must fight one after another. At this point I didn't know that this could lead to me getting my black belt. I was only fifteen and people didn't get their black belt until they were over sixteen.

. . . as a youth . . .

I won those three fights and suddenly every person in the sports hall was jumping up and down, screaming and shouting for me. I know this because I was told afterwards. I couldn't see or hear them because I wasn't there. I was somewhere else on my own, overwhelmed with every single emotion I could possibly imagine. I think I knew I must have done it but I couldn't believe I had achieved something that seemed almost impossible before that moment.

I discovered a new part of myself. I found that I was capable of winning in life and doing it without even knowing. Something inside me took over and drove me on to new heights.

. . . as a youth . . .

Unemployment

Being unemployed really helped me to realise a lot about myself and a lot about the people around me. Firstly I noticed I had become very withdrawn and not only this but I had got very angry and frustrated. This was when I realised how special all the people around me were, because all of these people were so supportive. I honestly don't know sometimes how they put up with me.

The worst times of all were when I had job interviews and then got turned down. A brave face couldn't contain all the frustration and I really did get very tetchy. I felt at times that nobody was interested in giving me a job, even though it was not always down to them personally. It was more circumstances. But at the time I wasn't prepared to accept that. I just got a complex and more depressed.

Also by this time I felt I had become a social outcast, which I think is the hardest thing to deal with. All my *friends*, on knowing I had lost my job, suddenly didn't seem to care. There were no invitations to go out, (which I couldn't have accepted anyway because I had no money), but also there were no invites to visit and no one visited me, except, as I mentioned earlier, my closest friends. One thing about losing a job is you really do find out who your real friends are.

This whole period in my life is something that I do not wish ever to go through again. It was four months until I found a job. My confidence was as low as could be and I was very bitter. Now I have been working again for a while and have begun once again to plan the future.

. . . as a youth . . .

When I became
a full-grown man,
time ran.

An adult's wish for a grandchild – 'the rare, the incomparable gift of time' – begins this section. Time seems to go so much faster when we are grown up and life can sweep people along in a headlong rush. 'No one can prepare you for the lack of time for yourself', writes the parent of a new-born baby. How can we 'come to terms with time', as the poet puts it? By learning to recognise the *moments of truth*, say the writers in this section: 'a few minutes with my little sons dissolve the anxieties and angers of the day'; 'someone was playing a harmonica – a man on his way to work, taking a moment, weighing it, finding its worth'; 'I can close my eyes and see it – just that one instance was a trigger'. Three people discover that it is not the length of time that matters, but the glimpses of something of great worth, not seen before, that come unexpectedly, in fleeting moments of time.

Prayer for a Grandchild

Let no-one hurry her Lord,
Give her the rare, the incomparable gift of time
Days to dream, dragonfly days, days when the kingfisher
Suddenly opens for her a window on wonder.
Let no-one chivvy her Lord; let her meander
Lark-happy through childhood, by fern bordered streams
Fringed butter yellow with kingcups; by secret ways
That paws have worn through the wild;
Give her cuckoo-land days and the owl's cry
By night.

Dear Lord, give her rainbows;
Show her a nest filled with sky-blue promises;
Scoop up the sounding oceans for her in a shell.
Let her keep her dreams
So that she will always turn her face to the light;
Live merrily, love well,
Hold out ungloved hands to flower and child.
Be easy with animals, come to terms with time.
Lord, let her keep her dreams;
Let her riches be remembered happy days.

Anon.

. . . full grown . . .

Parenthood

From the moment we knew we were expecting a baby life was full of excitement and apprehension. Each week that passed was a major milestone, one week nearer the birth and one week less of feeling unwell. As the end of the pregnancy approached the excitement got greater and time seemed to drag. However, this was nothing compared to how we felt when he arrived. How could we possibly be responsible for something so small, so helpless, so wonderful? We still find it difficult to believe he is part of us.

The feelings we have for Rhys are feelings we had never imagined, the joy when he first smiled or when he put his arms out to be picked up, the wonder at every achievement, however small. It can be difficult not to be too absorbed in it all. Parenthood is such a common event yet to us it was so amazing, starting a new life and taking the responsibility for the development of that life from the moment of conception to, well, when does it stop?

Along with the delight and excitement there are the constant concerns as to whether or not you are doing 'the right thing'. Parenthood is something for which you are given constant advice. Those who have had children and many who haven't tell you how and when to do things. To begin with we were constantly asking questions so that we could ensure we were doing things the very best way, but as our experience grew we quickly realised that other people's opinions didn't matter. What was important was that we felt happy with what we were doing. After all he is our baby and we know him better than anyone.

Then there are the endless broken nights. Everyone warns you, but no one can prepare you for how disruptive babies really are. It can be hard to be objective at 3 o'clock in the morning when you have been woken for maybe the second time, trying to stay calm and not be impatient, trying to remind yourself that they are not doing it on purpose. And no one can prepare you for the lack of time for yourself. No longer can you be sure of eating a meal or watching even the shortest television programme without being disturbed.

. . . full grown . . .

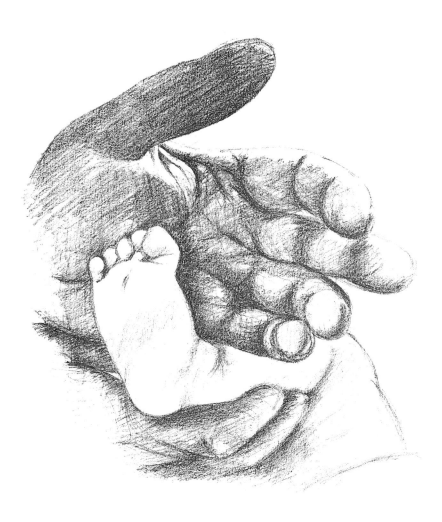

Having someone who is totally dependent on you is a daunting prospect, as is wondering how much to let go at each stage as he develops. The arrival of our son had a dramatic and wonderful effect on our lives. It takes time to adjust, but now we can't imagine life without him.

. . . full grown . . .

Young children

Young children change your life. For me the change has been
the most extraordinary and unexpected thing I can remember. I
could not say for certain, before I had them, that I wanted
children; and I surely did not feel ready for the responsibilities
and duties of a father and breadwinner. But I also had no
experience of the love and inspiration that young children
would bring me, and which would turn cares into pleasures. I
had no idea that a child could make me feel a wholeness I had
never known.

Young children show you how fruitless are so many of the
things and thoughts that concern us. A few minutes with my
little sons dissolves the anxieties and anger of the day. Nothing I
fret about on my own account is important when I see them;
their simplicity is a well of strength. Having them and loving
them, I have learned a little faith; a little glimpse of the stillness
and beauty that continues above and beyond my cares and
ambitions.

I have learned that there is this stillness and beauty in many
things; it has always been there, but I have not known how to
see it. I know now, because my children have taught me, to look
for it when I feel anxious or dull, a slave of routine, hard of
heart.

Taking a moment

One day, as I travelled to work, I felt a long way from the innocence of children. The previous day, a small boy had seen his mother assaulted and murdered in a London park. I could not shake off a fascinated horror at the image of this two-year-old child clinging to his mother's mutilated body and begging her to get up. Pity began to grow into bitterness, and anger. Everything about me seemed stained and worthless.

Trying, and failing, to raise myself I made my way into the gathering rush of London. Despair bore in on me with the commuter-crush. I took my place in the crowd that shuffled on to the escalator and began to descend into the tunnels, stifling in the summer heat. How many of us might be capable of such an act of brutality? We spilled on to the platform and stood shoulder to shoulder, waiting. In the stillness before the train rumbled through the tunnel from the next station, there was music. Somewhere among us someone was playing a harmonica; simple, graceful music played with skill, and seeming at odds with this crowded place, as if the player were sitting by the side of a cool stream on a fine evening. For some moments no one stirred. The train arrived; we boarded, crushing in, elbows in eyes. I looked back as the platform cleared; still the music played, and I saw a man in his thirties, Asiatic, well-dressed, sitting on a bench with a briefcase at his side; he showed no sign of moving to board the train. Not a busker; a man on his way to work, taking a moment, weighing it, and, alone of all of us, finding its worth.

The doors slammed shut and the train slid out of the station, leaving the music behind. Perhaps I was not the only one who had been reminded of something good, outside myself.

Why?

I think the one moment that stays the clearest in my mind would be when **The Conveyor** was hit – a very large ship. It was late afternoon and we were detailed to go and rescue those on board. I saw a great churning column of black smoke and as we got nearer and nearer I realised that a lot of people were in a lot of trouble.

As we got within a few hundred yards we could hear explosions within the ship and on the upper deck Chinook helicopters were being engulfed by flames. There were men with breathing apparatus running around, in what was now a futile gesture, attempting to put the flames out. I could hear people screaming and shouting. I realised they were going to have to abandon ship and we were, again a futile gesture, trying to spray water across the side of the ship.

The ladders were lowered down the side. There was a reasonable swell and there's quite a few feet from the deck down to the sea. Some men, in haste, attempted to jump from the top. I can still close my eyes and see one man, as he fell, catch his arm or his leg, and fall into the water.

A few minutes after that many of the men were in the water and there was a man a few yards away from me. I cut a length of rope and threw it to him. I was swearing at him to grab hold of the rope. He was still moving his arms about but obviously the cold water was getting to him. But there were a lot of other people in the water and somebody grasped my shoulder and said "leave him, he's dead." I just moved away, dropped the rope. I screamed. I was screaming out loud to the sky. I wasn't cursing the Argentinians. It was a real disgusting waste. I just saw it as that at that point.

I thought *why?* This man was probably a civilian on **The Conveyor**. I just couldn't believe that that had happened. It was – you know – and I'll never forget it. I can close my eyes and see it, and I think that just that one instance was a trigger. I wanted to know why from then on.

Reproduced with the permission of the Controller of HMSO and the BBC. The extract is taken from a programme in the series 'Two People' which was broadcast on BBC Radio 4 on 13th February 1992.

And later,
as I older grew,
time flew.

Time is a strange thing. Do we live in it, or create it? Sometimes there seems too much time, sometimes too little. When people grow older and step back a bit from everything that has kept them busy all their lives, time seems different again: it has 'a new spaciousness', says a writer here, there is room for thought and for seeing things more clearly – 'there is a sharpened awareness of what we have always seen but rarely noticed'. 'I cherish the memory of many very happy times in my life', writes another. After a long time away from home, someone else found 'everyone I met gave me such a great welcome, and I was suddenly aware these people were friends and how much they meant to me'. There is also a suggestion in this section that perhaps we do not have to stay within time: 'Now, perhaps for the first time, we may reach out, above and beyond ourselves, to look for pattern and meaning'. A writer in the book's last section says: 'There was a time when I was not and a time when I became'. What is the meaning of the period between birth and death which we call life, and which 'may be hours, weeks, months or many years...'?

When I retire...

For many, these words are a cornucopia of ambitions to fulfil, neglected friends to visit and longed for treats and holidays. It is as if life is 'on hold' and will only begin in earnest when retirement is reached.

As the time grew closer I found my perspective changed from looking forward to looking back. Over the years I had known so many children and their families, there were so many memories. I found myself on a path of *last times*, the last time I would ring the bell, the last time I would take assembly, the last time ... Although I had asked for no fuss, in the event I found the presentations, cards and flowers, so many flowers, a great joy and support for what is a major milestone in life. Retirement is, for most of us, very final. There is no going back. The world of work will go on without us, and the activities associated with retiring become rites of passage.

When retirement is, at last, a reality, life assumes new horizons. In spite of the fulfilment of some of those planned activities there is a new spaciousness of time for thought, a sharpened awareness of what we have always seen but rarely noticed. Did it always get dark so early in December, or the daffodils show through so soon after Christmas? 'Consider the lilies of the field'. In my case it was the winter flowering pansies. The rich burgundy, blues and yellows shone like beacons of hope, quickly reviving after the sharpest of frosts. Before, there had been so little time 'to stand and stare', or for what Yehudi Menuhin calls 'the unfamiliar delights of idleness'.

Well-meaning friends are now quick to suggest things to pass the time, but one of the greatest rewards of retirement is to have time – time to pause, time to think and to take stock. For three score years most of us will have been on a helter-skelter of experience but have made little time to reflect on it. We have felt the warmth of the sun and stood in the darkest shadows. We have come to know the heights and depths to which the human spirit can reach. Now, perhaps for the first time, we may reach out, above and beyond ourselves, to look for pattern and meaning.

. . . as I older grew . . .

Are all these for *me?*

I cherish the memory of many very happy times in my life, which these days would be called 'peak experiences':

the first Christmas which I recall – I must have been nearly three years old – I was amazed to be given so many presents: "Are these all for *me?*"

numerous visits to the seaside and the countryside, when I was enchanted by the colours and fragrance of the natural world;

the joy of singing when I was a chorister;

the quietly eager expectation as I prepared for my Confirmation and first Communion;

listening to music – from Bach to Brass Bands;

browsing in second-hand bookshops and sometimes finding a book I had been seeking for years;

times when the words of Stevenson seemed true –

The world is so full of a number of things,
I am sure we should all be as happy as kings.

On such life-enhancing occasions, I have wanted to say to the giver of all good – "Thank you! Thank you!"

. . . as I older grew . . .

Friendship

I have considered myself fortunate to have good friends around me but did not recognise the depth of these friendships until I was away for several months, leaving my home and garden in the care of others. I must admit I did not give much thought to those people whom I had left behind while I was on holiday.

However, on my return, I realised how much had been done for me in my absence. Also, apart from cards, flowers and greetings from neighbours, as I walked through the village shortly after my return home everyone I met gave me such a great welcome, and I was suddenly aware these people were friends and how much they meant to me. Friendship is intangible. You cannot buy it and it matures and builds up over time.

People who make friends as they advance through life will not be lonely in later years. It is important to keep a friendship alive and in constant repair and to be alert to changes. One should try to be patient with the faults and imperfections of others, and what appears unlikeable in a friend one should take care to correct in oneself.

We do not always recognise that we have true and honest friends until some trauma in life brings tremendous offers of comfort and support. Friends are there to call upon to help us in times of need. A hand that grasps you firmly, a hug or a pat on the back can give an uplift and feeling of support.

. . . as I older grew . . .

Soon shall I find, while travelling on, time gone.

Perhaps, eventually, the structure of time is no longer necessary to us. It has been like a map for a journey. In the last section of this book people reveal some of the discoveries they have made on the journey: 'My understanding is that Truth comes from God, and that by its very nature it must be God.' 'Something is planted deep into the human spirit... which can bring out the best in us in times of adversity.' 'I was aware of something which was other than self, but which, nevertheless, included it, in an experience of wholeness and love.' For many, *moments of truth* have been to do with recognising the need for love. In a book about how people try to understand life, a German writer says: '... once we have experienced the possibility of love, something remains behind in us called conscience. We know then that without love we are missing the essential.' That knowledge made a child writing in the first part of this book cry out "No!" when he heard his father was leaving home. It made the radar operator in the Falklands war 'scream out loud to the sky' at the 'real disgusting waste' of war, and wonder *why*? Conversely, another writer, speaking of his little sons, said: 'Having them and loving them, I have learned a little faith.' And another: 'It is the essential spirit and love which was him which is present with me now.' Asking 'What is this love?' the German writer says it is *seeing*, a *seeing* which transforms people. The contributors to **Moments of Truth** describe some of the transformations they have experienced.

Life never stands still

I'm glad there is movement in the title of the last section of the book for I have learnt to accept that life never stands still. All is change, we are surrounded by it and we are ourselves changing moment by moment. We are woven into time and become part of all we have met on the journey. Time can be used as a measurement which divides life up into past, present and future and if we are not careful we carry the past with us and waste time planning for the future. We don't *live* in the present where the moments of truth are. Consequently we are not aware of them – we miss them.

It is in a moment of awareness that one is lifted out of time on to another level. I had this experience when driving alone across the Transvaal in South Africa. I was aware of the road ahead and the great ball of shining light coming up over the horizon, the stony barren land on either side and the great expanse of cloudless sky above. For a moment I had a wonderful feeling of *unity* with all that *is*. Time was being suspended and there was only *being*. I was unaware that I was travelling at speed and there was nothing to remind me of history, civilization, religions, or birth and death as we know them. It is impossible to describe the moment within me for in a sense the self was not there. I was aware of something which was other than self, but which, nevertheless, included it, in an experience of wholeness and love.

I think our difficulty is with time. We live in time and it divides our life and thoughts into little bits which then war with each other. I ask myself can we, as travellers, live without these divisions – in the present – from moment to moment. Time is movement and brings change but it is made up of individual moments. It is in these that truth may break in on us and change our perspectives.

The essential spirit

I waited a long time to get married. Although opportunities presented themselves none of them seemed quite right and I became resigned to living alone. When I met A, I knew within a very short space of time that I wanted to be with him. And in being with him he allowed me to be – to relax into who I was, whilst being enriched by the joy of who he was – our complimentary personalities fused in a way I had never imagined possible and life became joyous through just being me and knowing him. In one man I found my best friend, my lover, my father, my son and … my husband. The knowledge that everybody else loved him too was a bonus. Only one cloud hovered on our horizon – he was many years older than I. Even that had its positive side as we tried to squeeze the maximum into our shared time together. We travelled, we saw friends, we swam, we enjoyed music and theatre and above all else we revelled in each other's company. We were eighteen again and there was no age difference between us.

But we weren't eighteen and he had reached a time in his life when his journey was to become one without me. One night without warning he walked upstairs to join me in our favourite room and collapsed at my feet. However much in my frenzy I implored him to "*live, please live!*" his time was ripe and our paths were to separate. I shall always consider it a great privilege that I was with him when he died.

And now? The last seven months have been extraordinary in every sense but through the unbearable pain and heartache of being without him physically yet I am not alone. I knew when I kissed him for the last time that the man I loved was no longer within his body. It is the essential spirit and love which was him which is present with me now. Everything he gave me and that we shared in our six years together is alive and sustaining me in my path ahead. It is not the lonely path trodden before our meeting. I am living for the two of us now. I am his representative and that is not only fulfilling but a gift. People said how lucky we were to meet and know such happiness. That was true in his lifetime and remains true now.

... travelling on ...

Waiting

There was a time when I was not and a time when I became. This entry into a world of time and space is a common experience of every human being. From the moment of birth we move toward the moment of death – the period in between is what we call life. It may be hours, weeks, months or many years. Its duration varies with every individual as does its quality. We may think we understand others but our understanding is only partial, because no two human beings are the same. Each is unique. I think it was the growing awareness of this fact that really convinced me of the existence of that presence, or force, in all things, which mankind calls God.

At the approaching end of a long life, I sometimes wonder whether I have made much progress at all. A good deal of time has been spent in unlearning, or throwing off, things which in my youth I accepted unquestioningly, and I realise how very little I really know and how much energy I have used on things which now seem non-essential. But perhaps it is good to be able to discard long-cherished viewpoints without regret.

As age overtakes me arthritis restricts my mobility, but I am in no way unhappy. I become increasingly aware of the heaven within. Remember Our Lord's words, 'The Kingdom of God is within you.' Whilst experience of heaven will undoubtedly be expanded when we take our leave of this world it does come to us all at the most unexpected of times and in the most unlikely of places, in friends, in faces, in kindness, in animals and birds, in nature at large. We are lifted from the world into the spiritual realm. And whilst in one sense I am waiting for God, there is a sense in which I come to a deeper awareness and experience of him as the days and weeks go by.

In Tagore's Gitanjali I read, 'Because I love this life I know I shall love death as well.' But I have to say I do so with some slight reservation. Because I love this life so much, I hope I shall love death as well, praying hard that when twilight gives way to nightfall, hope will give way to certainty.

Inner peace

Life is a journey. As we travel, many of us are conscious of a feeling that something or someone is gently trying to lead us to a position where we feel content and at peace within ourselves. As a youngster I had all sorts of plans and ambitions about what I was going to do and become. Time came to leave childhood and school behind and enter the realm of the workplace, only to find I had to take what employment was offered and within my capabilities. Past ambitions were shattered. Later, a growing sense of discontent and restlessness forced me to think of how to escape the trap I seemed to be in. Unknown to me, help was at hand. I became redundant.

The end of the world? Not so! Another job came along, and with it a sense of relief that surely my inner restlessness must now be cured. After a while I began to have the familiar old feeling again, but this time also a realisation of what the trouble was. 'This is not the work I really should be doing.' So I found one part of me saying 'here are all life's needs available to you if you stick with this job', while another part said 'may be, but you will never be at peace with yourself until you find your true vocation.'

My moment of truth came to me early one morning as I got ready to go to work. The inner pressures had increased and I had tried to kill them off by means of all kinds of activities. I had become quite certain where I was being led by those interior pressures and I did not like the idea. Then came that moment of truth when, out of sheer frustration with this constant pressure, I said to no one in particular 'Oh, all right, I will do it.' From that moment the inner pressure ceased.

What was this moment of truth? Where did it come from? For what purpose? My understanding is that ultimately Truth comes from God, and that by its very nature it must be God. It seems, if this is true, that God was within me making himself known as a kind of pressure or presence, because he wanted me to do something to which, if it was to happen, I had to agree. The end choice was mine. All this moment of truth, moment of God, wanted from me were those simple words 'I will', thus giving to God all that I am which is his true worth.

"What a good thing..."

'Time gone' has muted the shock that almost broke us when, through a car accident, our twelve-year-old daughter, Lesley, became a quadraplegic. When, after operations and rehabilitation, she finally returned home, we, her parents and younger sister, Jacqueline, had to completely reorganise our lives. It sounds strange, but it is true, to say that in the four and a half years that followed we had a happy, rewarding time together. We came to know what living was all about. Nothing was taken for granted. Each day became something for which to be grateful. Fortunately we were surrounded by the prayerful fellowship and practical help of friends and relatives, for how could we have coped alone?

But were we ever alone in the true sense of that word? As we look at our world today we are constantly reminded of the way in which ordinary people rise above their terrible circumstances. Something is planted deep into the human spirit by God – or whatever name you prefer to call its originator – which can bring out the best in us in times of adversity. Those who ignore this source of help – usually channelled through others – often succumb to bitterness and despair. Children, particularly, exhibit the strength of this God-force in their shattered lives. This was underlined for us when our helpless daughter, watching her lively sister cavorting around, said, "What a good thing this didn't happen to Jacqueline."

We lived in the constant shadow of death during those years but Lesley, helped by this inner spirit, taught us to face each day normally. And when the day came that her weakened frame succumbed to infection, and she died peacefully, there was a living presence in her room of which I, the least imaginative of people, was acutely aware. We were given the comfort and knowledge that she had been gathered up into a happier sphere. Any fear of death we might previously have had went and when my husband died some years later Jacqueline said, "Isn't it wonderful to know that daddy and Lesley are together again?" I am convinced that what matters most is our personal response to what happens in our lives, because this is what leads us either forward into light and ultimately into 'true' worship – or backwards into darkness.

Endpiece

Where truth prevails

Men make their god in Time's image,
Raise his shrine in every land,
Order their lives to a clock's ticking,
Live and die at his command.

How swift is life on such a reckoning!
Years pass like a driven cloud:
Only a breath, and generations
Exchange their cot-clothes for a shroud.

Love lies under the clock's ticking:
Be still, and know another God.
One moment freed from Time's dominion
Exceeds a year from his measuring-rod.

Mortals, seek that immortal moment!
Crucified by Time's twelve nails
I cannot hasten as man hastens,
And stillness teaches where truth prevails.

From Sundial.